The History and Mystery of
STONEHENGE

by **Jan Goldberg**

The History and Mystery of Stonehenge
by Jan Goldberg

Illustrations by Dan Bridy
Photography: p.iv © Richard T. Nowitz/CORBIS; p.1 © Jason Hawkes/CORBIS;
p.8 top © Stapleton Collection/CORBIS; p.8 bottom © Sarah Jackson;
Edifice/CORBIS; p.12 © Bettmann/CORBIS; p.22 © John Wilkinson;
Ecoscene/CORBIS; p.23 © Chinch Gryniewicz; Ecoscene/CORBIS; p.33 ©
Bettmann/CORBIS; p.34 © Kevin Schafer/CORBIS; p.38 © Kevin Schafer/CORBIS;
p.39 © Richard T. Nowitz/CORBIS; p.43 © Adam Woolfitt/CORBIS; p.46 © Richard
T. Nowitz/CORBIS; p.47 © Roger Ressmeyer/CORBIS; p.50 © Reuters NewMedia
Inc./CORBIS; p.51 © Bettmann/CORBIS; p.52 © Greenhalf Photography/CORBIS;
p.59 © Colin Garratt; Milepost 92 1 2/CORBIS; p.61 © Angelo Hornak/CORBIS;
p.64 © Adam Woolfitt/Woodfin Camp/PictureQuest; p.66 © Adam Woolfitt/CORBIS;
p.68 top © Reuters NewMedia Inc./CORBIS; p.68 bottom © Angelo Hornak/CORBIS

Nonfiction Reviewer
John Barell, Ed.D.
Educational Consultant, The American Museum of Natural History
New York City

Design, Production, and Art Buying by
Inkwell Publishing Solutions, Inc., New York City
Cover Design by
Inkwell Publishing Solutions, Inc., New York City

ISBN: 0-7367-1789-7
Copyright © Zaner-Bloser, Inc.

Zaner-Bloser, Inc., P.O. Box 16764, Columbus, Ohio 43216-6764, 1-800-421-3018

Printed in China

03 04 05 06 07 (321) 5 4 3 2 1

TABLE OF CONTENTS

▲ The stones that survive at Stonehenge today ▶

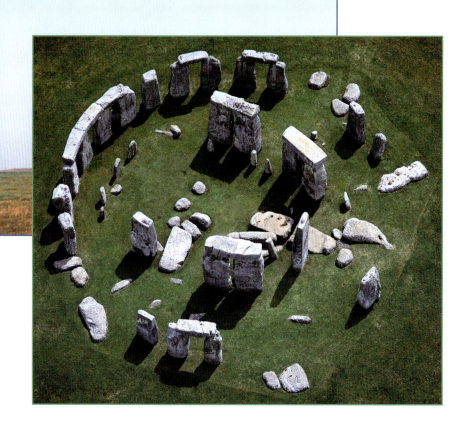

CHAPTER ONE
The Splendor of Stonehenge

It's dark and hazy, and you can barely see them. As you move toward them, you feel the deep, green grass beneath your feet. You close and open your eyes several times, thinking they'll disappear. But they're still there—stones, huge stones—all in a circle. It looks like a meeting of stone giants. These structures would dwarf the tallest basketball player. Though the wind is blowing, nothing is moving. All is still.

Your journey began earlier in the evening. A friend showed you a photo of this truly unusual place. She brought it back from a recent trip. The place is called Stonehenge. You thought about what it might be like to visit there. Could you be dreaming?

Stonehenge is known all over the world. Year after year, it is the most popular visitor site in Great Britain. Created centuries ago, this **ceremonial** ruin is a national symbol.

This monument is a series of earth, timber, and stone arrangements. It is circled by a wall of earth. The stone structures were built, arranged, and rearranged over a period of 1,000 to 2,000 years.

The size of these stones is hard to grasp. Some of them weigh up to 40 tons each. That is about as much as 30 cars! The stones are 20 to 30 feet tall. They would tower over four people standing on one another's shoulders.

It's amazing that ancient people were able to plan, organize, and carry out such a huge project. Remember, they didn't have the modern tools and instruments we have today. Truly, Stonehenge is proof of the cleverness and strength of its builders. It also clearly shows their determination.

The When and Where of Stonehenge

The construction of Stonehenge began 4,000 to 5,000 years ago. Can you imagine the skill it would take to build something that would endure for that long? That's what happened with Stonehenge. The builders must have had very good reasons to build such a sturdy structure. They also must have been very dedicated.

Stonehenge was built on Salisbury Plain in southern England. It is 30 miles from the English Channel and 80

▲ Stonehenge is in southern England.

miles from London. Stonehenge stands on an open **down**.
A down is a gently rolling plain. Stonehenge seems to
stand alone. However, at one time, it was part of a
network of monuments. You can read more about that in
Chapter Seven.

We don't know why this area was selected as the site
for this huge monument. The choice is even more
surprising because of the soil here. Only a few inches

below the surface, you will find a substance like chalk. Chalk provides a very unstable foundation for building. The builders must have had an important reason for selecting this site. However, we can only guess what it might have been.

An Architectural Wonder

Many stone monuments were created all over Europe during these early times. About 50,000 of them still exist. They are called **megaliths**. This term is based on a Greek word that means "great stone."

However, of all these stone wonders, many experts agree that Stonehenge is the most outstanding. For one thing, its stones were carefully shaped to different sizes. They were also placed in special patterns. They were fitted together using methods we still use today.

Christopher Witcombe is an expert on Stonehenge. He is in charge of the art history department at Sweet Briar College in Virginia. Witcombe believes that ancient people went through a period when they put stones into various positions and patterns. In this way, they created many monuments. Still, compared to the other stone monuments, Stonehenge is special.

Stonehenge would be an amazing achievement in any time. However, it was built during the Late Stone and Early Bronze ages. Back then, people did not have any of the construction tools we have today. They were just beginning to understand how to use the wheel.

"The very fact that they (the stones) have survived must mean they are special in some way," says Witcombe. "The builders went to a lot of trouble to find the stones. Then they had to carry the stones to this certain place. That shows how important that spot was to them."

It's not just the stones that make it special. It's a spot that was already special for some reason.

Many Secrets

One of the many secrets relating to Stonehenge is who coined its name. Some say it was the Saxons. This group of people lived during the second century. The meaning of *Stonehenge* is also a mystery. It might have come from words that mean "circle of stones," "hanging stones," or "stone hinges."

Stonehenge holds many other secrets. There were no written languages at the time, so we have no written record that tells us how and why Stonehenge was built. Archaeologists have to find other records. Some answers are hidden in the ground. They are waiting to be unearthed in scraps of bone, pottery, stone shavings, and pieces of burnt carbon. If an object was left on the ground near Stonehenge 100 years ago, it would be buried six to eight inches below the surface today!

Many questions surround this monument. They have kept the mystery of Stonehenge alive for thousands of years. During this time, countless astronomers, archaeologists, and engineers have been studying Stonehenge. So have historians and other researchers.

Still, many questions remain. Who created this monument? What were their daily lives like? Why did they choose this site? How were the stones moved from one place to another? How was the monument built? How did someone organize the hundreds of people who must have been involved? Who was in charge? Why did generations of workers keep working on this huge undertaking? Most importantly, why was Stonehenge built at all?

As you read about the mysteries of Stonehenge, think about the questions you have. Maybe you'll find the answers here. Perhaps someday you will want to research this topic more. You may do the research yourself, make new discoveries, and maybe answer other people's questions.

A Shadow of Yesterday

Only the ruins of Stonehenge stand today. They give us just a glimpse of the original monument. Many stones are missing or leaning. Some lie broken on the ground. Still, archaeologists have studied these clues. They pieced together what the original monument probably looked like.

Stonehenge reveals many truths about early civilizations. At the same time, it guards many secrets about those civilizations. Continuing advances in technology will help us learn more about Stonehenge.

These advances will also help us learn more from Stonehenge. The world will be watching as more of its secrets are revealed.

◀ This drawing shows what Stonehenge might have looked like centuries ago.

▲ Today's Stonehenge is bathed in the rising sun.

CHAPTER TWO
Determining the Age of Stonehenge

Did you ever dig up something in your backyard? Did you wonder how old it was? Did you wonder how long it had been there? How do researchers figure out the age of something they unearth?

In the case of Stonehenge, scientists have determined that it has existed for thousands of years. They have also determined the likely sequence of events that resulted in Stonehenge. How do they know this? Scientists spend much time researching, and then verifying the results.

Much of the information about Stonehenge is new. It was not until the twentieth century that we were able to obtain reliable information about Stonehenge. We have now identified its main features. Experts still disagree about details. However, we are fairly certain when the parts of Stonehenge were built. We have a good idea of the order in which they were constructed.

Two main techniques have allowed us to uncover this information. They are **excavation** and **radiocarbon dating**.

Excavation

An excavation is a hole that has been carefully dug. The goal is to preserve any objects that are found. Then those objects are studied.

Archaeologists have patiently dug around the stones of Stonehenge. They have also studied large areas of the Salisbury Plain. In their search, they have found ancient tools. They also dug up jewelry and weapons. These objects had been buried for centuries. As they dug, scientists unearthed the ashes of human bodies. The ashes had been buried in bags made from animal skins.

These discoveries provided valuable information. They indicated that Stonehenge was built in three phases. The objects also showed that it had been built by different groups of people over a very long period.

These are drawings ▶ of the types of tools that have been found at Stonehenge.

As they dug, scientists unearthed layers of ashes from fires. The ashes of some fires lay on top of the ashes from other fires. The ashes underneath must have been from fires built earlier. This evidence helps prove that Stonehenge was built at different times. Most experts estimate that its construction took between 1,000 and 2,000 years and that it was started earlier than originally thought.

Radiocarbon Dating

A turning point came in the late 1940s. After that, scientists no longer had to guess the age of Stonehenge. An American chemist, Willard Libby, discovered radiocarbon dating in 1949. This technique determines the age of materials that were once alive. That includes bone, skin, hair, grains and grass as well as paper, cloth, and charcoal. (Charcoal is made from burned wood. Some plants rot away and cannot be studied, but charcoal remains for a long period.)

A tiny fraction of the carbon on the earth is radioactive. When living things die, this radiocarbon, or carbon 14, decays at a known rate. By measuring how much carbon 14 remains in an organic material, scientists can calculate how long ago death occurred.

Let's use a tree that once grew at Stonehenge as an example. When the tree is alive, the amount of carbon 14 is continually renewed from the atmosphere. However, when it dies, the carbon 14 begins to decay and is released into the air as nitrogen. The carbon 14 is not replenished.

▲ Dr. Willard Libby stands next to equipment that helps
scientists to measure the rate of decay of carbon 14. Then
they know how long ago a living thing died.

When archaeologists find a sample of wood or charcoal
from the tree at Stonehenge, they can send it to a lab to
determine the amount of carbon 14 left.

By measuring the rate of decay of carbon 14, scientists
can tell how much time has passed since the death of the
tree. One half of the carbon 14 atoms will decay every
5,760 years. This is called the "half-life" of carbon. Given
this information, scientists can determine how much of the
carbon 14 is left in the wood. Then they can figure out
how old it is.

Using this date, scientists then can figure out when the
stone closest to the wood was moved. Scientists have

determined which groups of people lived near Stonehenge during certain periods. So the age of the wood also tells them which group of people probably have raised the stone.

Radiocarbon Dating at Stonehenge

Scientists used radiocarbon dating on a deer antler found at Stonehenge. They believe the antler was used as a pick during the first phase of Stonehenge's construction. **Carbon dating** indicates that the first phase took place around 3100 B.C. They now call this period Stonehenge I.

Based on the evidence, the builders probably began this huge monument work in a simple way. They pounded a stake into the ground. This would be the center of Stonehenge. Next, they tied a long rope to the stake. Then they pulled the end of the rope around the stake, making

▲ When a living thing dies, it begins to release carbon 14 into the air as nitrogen.

13

a circle. They might have used a deer antler to mark the circle. The next step was digging a deep pit around the circle. They might have used the shoulder blades of oxen as shovels. In this way, the construction of Stonehenge began.

Using radiocarbon dating, scientists made a discovery. Stonehenge is older than people once thought. Strangely enough, the construction of a parking lot for visitors led to this discovery. Three holes were uncovered during this construction. In them, scientists found pieces of charcoal, pine, and burnt bone. They determined the age of these pieces. Then they changed their estimates of the age of Stonehenge.

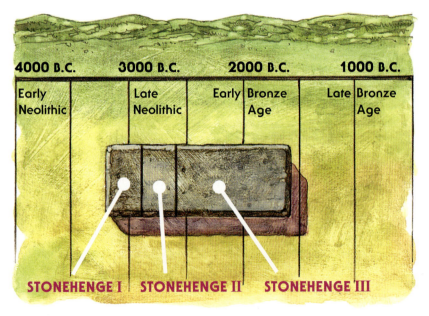

▲ Not everyone agrees on the dates for the three phases of Stonehenge, but this is a widely accepted time line.

Chapter Three
The Building of Stonehenge: Phases I and II

You have already learned that the parts of Stonehenge were built during different periods. This is also true of a number of ancient churches and cathedrals. Most experts agree that construction of Stonehenge began around 3100–3000 B.C. It lasted until about 1600–1500 B.C. This means that building continued for about 15 centuries. However, experts question what took place during each stage.

Some scientists even add a Pre-Stonehenge period to the time line. During this time, they believe that at least four large pits were dug. They are in a line about 218 yards from the site. At one time, pine posts were placed in the pits. No one knows the purpose of these posts.

Stonehenge I

Remember that we have no written records of this prehistoric time. Still, people want to know when the construction of Stonehenge began. Some scientists studied the position of the stones to determine the start of construction. They believed that Stonehenge was built to face the sunrise on the **solstice**. (Summer solstice is the longest day of the year. Winter solstice is the shortest day of the year.) However, their estimates of the start of construction varied widely. Their ideas were not well accepted.

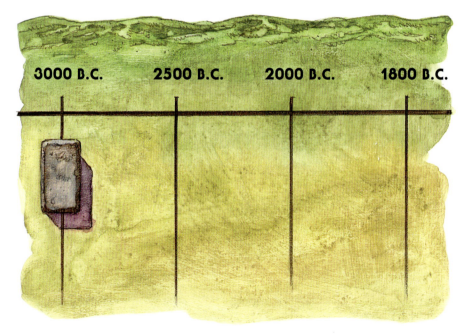

3000 B.C.   2500 B.C.   2000 B.C.   1800 B.C.

▲ Many—but not all—experts accept this time line for Stonehenge I.

Much of our knowledge about Stonehenge I is based on objects found in the soil. You have already read about the carbon dating of a deer antler found buried at Stonehenge. This information has been used to pinpoint the time of Stonehenge I. It occurred about 3100–2900 B.C.

Phase I of Stonehenge is sometimes called the "earthwork monument." Evidence has shown that Stonehenge started as a circle. The circle was created by digging a **ditch**. The chalky soil from the ditch was piled

▲ Stonehenge begins.

up inside the circle. It formed a 6-foot-high, circular **bank** of earth. The circle measured 280 to 330 feet across. It was 5 to 7 feet deep. Just inside the earth bank was a circle of 56 holes, named Aubrey Holes, after John Aubrey who first observed them. At one time, each hole probably held a wooden post.

The Aubrey Holes were round pits in the chalky soil. Each pit was about a yard wide and a yard deep. It had steep sides and a flat bottom. Animal-skin bags filled with human ashes have been found in these holes. This discovery has greatly interested scientists. At least part of Stonehenge may have been used as a burial ground.

Some experts also believe that a wooden fence may have surrounded the site. Two large stones might have been placed to the northeast to mark an entryway. A smaller southern entrance might have also existed. Most experts believe that there were no structures in the center of Stonehenge during this time.

Might there be other possibilities? What do you think?

Phase II

After Phase I, some scientists believe that work on Stonehenge stopped for the next 200 years. No one is sure of the reason. Work did not continue until a new group of people, called the Beaker Folk, moved to Salisbury Plain. (The Beaker Folk were named for the drinking cups they made. You can read more about them in Chapter Five.)

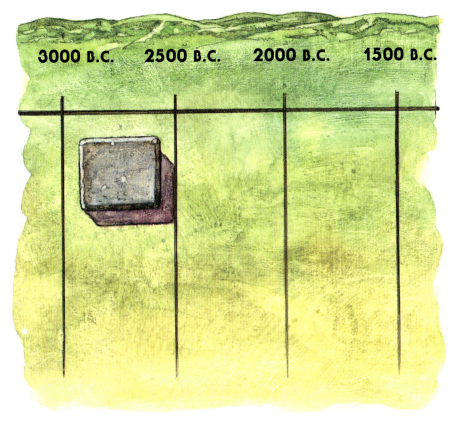

3000 B.C. 2500 B.C. 2000 B.C. 1500 B.C.

▲ Stonehenge II was built between 2900 B.C. and 2600 B.C.

Many experts feel that the second phase of Stonehenge started around 2900 B.C. and lasted three to five centuries. Phase II is called the "timber monument." During this time, workers built a complex design of timber posts. They may have been just rows of posts or solid wooden walls. Some of the posts might have formed a special **corridor** or hallway. The rising sun would have shone through this corridor on summer solstice, or midsummer's day.

19

The walls might also have kept people out of certain areas of Stonehenge. Perhaps those areas were special. We are not certain of the purpose or placement of the timbers. The wood rotted away long ago. Many of the holes may have been filled, purposely or accidentally. We don't always know for certain. This is the nature of scientific discovery.

During Phase II, Stonehenge was probably used as a cemetery. Bodies were burned, and their ashes were buried there. In fact, human ashes have been found in the Aubrey Holes.

Again, our information is very limited. Timber poles were probably added inside of the ditch and bank. No one is sure about their appearance or purpose. We know more about timber settings used in other regions of the world during this time. They were used to display tribal markers. Some were like totem poles. Perhaps these were, too.

CHAPTER FOUR
The Building of Stonehenge: Phase III

Experts believe that Phase III of Stonehenge took centuries to complete. It involved finding the stones, preparing them, and arranging them. This phase is called the "stone monument." Because prehistoric people had no machines, horses, or carts, building Stonehenge was a remarkable achievement. Can you imagine moving such gigantic stones without these things? The hard-working builders had to rely mostly on their own muscles. Their only tools were ropes, levers, and rollers.

The Bluestones

Phase III began about 2600 B.C. That's when workers brought 60 to 85 bluestones to the site. Four kinds of bluestone were used in Stonehenge. They were all formed from volcanic lava, an **igneous** rock. The colors range from greenish blue, to bluish gray, to dark olive green. One kind of bluestone is spotted with white or pink. Each stone was about 8 feet tall and 6.5 feet long. It weighed about 4 tons. That is about the weight of a female elephant!

▲ The Prescelly (also spelled Preseli) Mountains are the likely source of the bluestones found at Stonehenge.

When Stonehenge was built, there were no bluestones nearby. The bluestones most likely came from the Prescelly Mountains. These mountains are in southwest Wales. That is 240 miles from Stonehenge!

How did the builders manage to get the bluestones to Stonehenge? What do you think they used to do it? Most likely, they dragged and floated them there. The first part of the trip would have been overland. It was 15 to 25 miles from the mountains to the coast. During this time, the stones could have been dragged on **sledges** made of heavy logs.

▲ More bluestones

Rollers would have been placed under the sledges to allow them to slide forward. After the sledge moved over some rollers, the workers would have picked up the rollers behind the sledge and put them back in front of the sledge. In this way, the same rollers were used over and over.

Many men would have been needed to push and pull the heavy stones onto the sledges. Hundreds more would have pushed and pulled the sledges along the rollers. It probably took a whole day for 80 men to move one stone one mile. That means it would have taken almost six years to move the bluestones from the mountains just to the coast!

▲ The builders of Stonehenge probably dragged the stones on wooden rollers.

Probably many more than 80 men worked at this task. Still, it was a great challenge. Maybe the workers tackled this part of the project during winter. Why? When the ground was covered with snow and ice the ground would have been frozen solid. With no muddy roads, the sledges would have slid along more easily.

Upon reaching the coast, the stones would have been loaded onto rafts. Then they would float along the coast and down the river toward Stonehenge. The water part of the trip would most likely have been planned during the summer. Then the seas were calmer, and the weather was, in general, better.

The rafts would have taken the stones as close as possible to the construction site. The stones still would have to be hauled overland for another six miles. Then they were floated down another river. Finally, they had to be dragged for another two miles.

No other stone circle in Great Britain used stones from farther away than five or six miles. It's easy to understand why!

The water route would have added many miles to the trip. Still, it would have been much easier than carrying the stones the entire 240 miles over uneven ground.

Why didn't the builders use stones that were close by? Why did they risk their lives to bring these bluestones 25 miles overland and 215 miles over stormy seas? What do you think? Perhaps they believed the bluestones had magical powers. Perhaps the stones had some religious

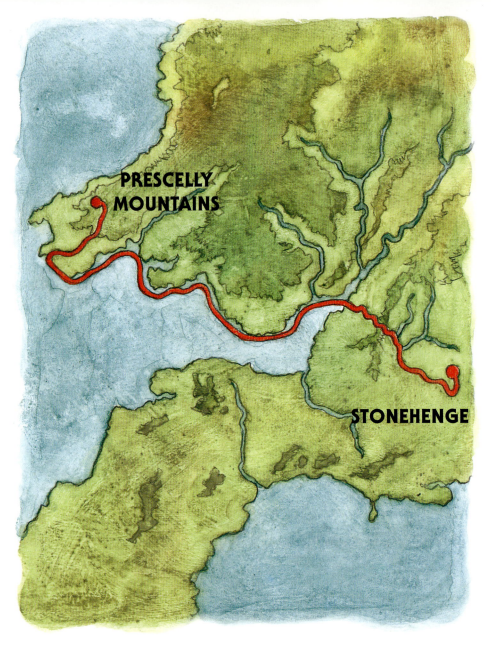

PRESCELLY
MOUNTAINS

STONEHENGE

▲ Overland or by water, the trip from the Prescelly Mountains
to Stonehenge was a long one.

meaning. Perhaps the builders believed the stones could cure disease. Maybe they had another reason that we haven't even guessed. We just don't know!

It is possible that these bluestones had been left near Salisbury Plain by a glacier. That could have taken place during a time long ago. However, not many experts think this happened. Instead, they believe that the stones were dragged and floated hundreds of miles for reasons we do not understand.

Most experts believe that the bluestones were arranged and rearranged several times. This went on for hundreds of years. In the end, the builders created a bluestone circle in the center of Stonehenge. It originally consisted of about 60 stones placed close together.

A second arrangement, called the bluestone horseshoe, was probably created later. It originally had 19 stones. They increased in height toward the center. Each stone had been shaped into a square pillar or a tapering **obelisk**. The two shapes alternate around the horseshoe.

The Sarsen Stones

The bluestones were big, but the sarsen stones were mammoth. *Sarsen* is a form of sandstone, a **sedimentary** rock. Each sarsen stone at Stonehenge weighs 25 to 50 tons! Now we're talking about the weight of about 10 elephants! The sarsen stones were brought from the Marlborough Downs. That is 20 miles north of Stonehenge.

Because of their weight, it's hard to believe that the sarsen stones were brought over water. Then how were they brought to Stonehenge? It's more likely that they were dragged overland. Still, that would have required massive sledges and rollers. It is possible that oxen helped in this work.

Over most of the likely route, the slopes are fairly flat. However, one stretch is rather steep. Can you imagine what it would have been like moving those stones uphill? Pulling the heaviest stone up this hill would have required about 500 people. An extra 100 to 200, at least, would have been needed to lay the rollers in front of the sledge. They also had to keep the sledge from sliding sideways. Even with all these people involved, the job could have taken more than a year to complete!

The Sarsen Circle

Finally, the builders at Stonehenge turned their attention to arranging the sarsens. They created the sarsen circle. It was 100 feet across. The circle originally consisted of 30 upright sarsen stones. Each weighed 25 tons or more. Each was about 7 feet wide, 3 to 4 feet thick, and 18 feet tall. Today, most of the sarsens are covered with grayish-green lichen, an organism consisting of fungus that grows on rocks and trees. It hides the original brightness of the stones. At the time they were raised, the stones would have been a mixture of blue, gray, green, and pearly pink.

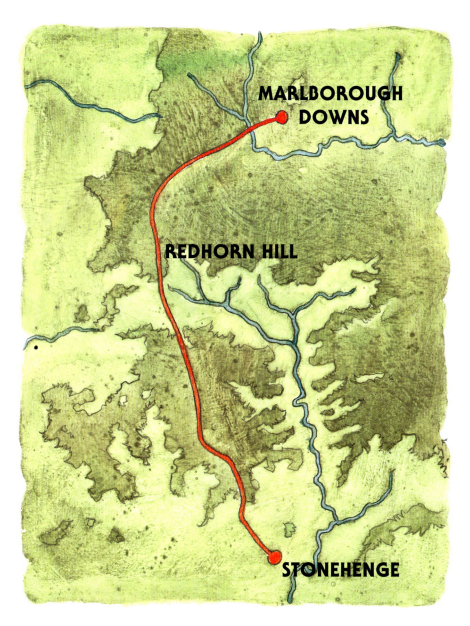

MARLBOROUGH DOWNS

REDHORN HILL

STONEHENGE

▲ The route of the sarsen stones was even longer and more difficult than that of the bluestones.

29

▲ Putting one sarsen stone into place was not easy. Most likely, the workers began by digging a pit. Then they drove in a row of wooden stakes to help steady the stone. Next, they moved the stone to the ramp, using rollers. Then each sarsen might have been pulled upright with ropes. It might have required 200 people to raise a stone into place.

The Lintels

Laid across the tops of the circle of 30 sarsens were smaller sarsen stones. They were called **lintels**. A circle of lintels resting on top of sarsens was unique to Stonehenge.

Each lintel weighed about 7 tons. It was only about one-fourth of the weight of a larger sarsen but still massive. It was also much smaller: 10.5 feet long, 3.5 feet wide, and 2.5 feet thick.

Raising the lintels into place was challenging. How might this have been done? Most likely, the lintel was first placed at the base of the uprights. As each end was lifted with levers, workers built a wooden framework underneath it. Slowly workers added layers to the framework, raising the lintel higher and higher. After many layers were built, the lintel was finally high enough. It was placed on top of the sarsens.

The lintels were not simply laid on the sarsens. On the top of each sarsen, the builders carved two knobs, about six inches across and three inches high. On the bottom of the lintels, they carved pits that fit snugly over the knobs. The knobs held the lintels in place.

The lintels were then joined together. A vertical groove was carved into one side of each lintel. A projection was carved out of the next lintel. Thus, each lintel slid into the groove on the next lintel. These methods were used to keep Stonehenge intact. However, of the original 30 lintels, 2 lie in pieces on the ground, 6 remain in place, and 22 are missing.

Placing one lintel required many workers and a very long time. ▼

◄ The lintels were attached to the upright sarsens and to each other.

Inside the sarsen circle, the builders also created a horseshoe of five sarsen **trilithons**. Each trilithon included two upright sarsens. Each sarsen weighed up to 45 tons. The builders also placed a lintel on each pair of sarsens. The tallest trilithon was in the center of the horseshoe. Called the Great Trilithon, it was 24 feet tall.

▲ Here is one of the impressive trilithons. Stonehenge workers built five of them inside the sarsen circle.

Only the inner surfaces of the trilithons were polished. Perhaps whatever took place inside the horseshoe was more important than what took place outside of it.

Shaping the Stones

Both the tall sarsen pillars and the smaller bluestones were shaped by months of pounding. This process is called **dressing** the stone. The workers needed to square off, round, or taper the stones. They also pounded the inner surfaces of the sarsens until they were smooth and polished. They probably used a heavy hammer about the size of a football.

The stones of Stonehenge were shaped with great skill and care. Each stone was slightly curved so the human eye would see it as perfectly straight. The ancient Greeks also used this eye-fooling technique in their columns. They built the Parthenon in 500 B.C. using this method. Strangely, no other monument built after Stonehenge was shaped with such care. It is clear that the builders of Stonehenge knew a great deal about engineering.

▲ This rock has been hammered into shape. It no longer has the rough surface of the natural stone.

34

SHAPING THE STONES

▲ To make a stone break at a certain place, the builders first pounded in a wedge. Next, they heated the stone. Then they poured cold water into the crack. A large stone would then split because of the sudden change in temperature.

▲ Smaller stones were probably used to hit and break the large pillars. These smaller stones might have weighed as much as 60 pounds.

▲ Workers also pounded stone wedges into a crack, prying it open. Then they forced wooden wedges into the crack. Water was poured over the wood, making it swell. As the wood expanded, it would split the stone.

▲ To grind away sharp edges, workers pushed and pulled one stone back and forth across another. Sand was mixed with water and spread between the two surfaces. This mixture sped up the grinding.

Carvings on the Stones

Several sarsen uprights have carvings on them. The carvings make Stonehenge even more interesting. The earliest of these is on one trilithon in the horseshoe. The carving is a shallow, oblong shape. It is similar to carvings found in stone burial chambers in Brittany. This carving is high above the ground. It was probably made before the stone was set in place.

The carvings on the other stones are closer to the ground. They were probably done after the stones had been placed. Most of them are drawings of bronze ax-heads from an early time. This type of carving was common from about 1800 B.C. to 1500 B.C. It has been found in Britain and Ireland.

▲ This drawing represents the carvings on the most decorated sarsens.

One carving might represent a foreign bronze dagger. It is similar to the kind found in an area of Greece. We may never know for sure the meanings of these carvings. However, they must have had a special meaning to the people of the time. What do you think they might represent?

▲ In its final form, the main part of Stonehenge consisted of the sarsen circle and the horseshoe of trilithons.

Other Important Structures at Stonehenge

Stonehenge also offers many other interesting structures. They include the Avenue, the Station Stones, the Slaughter Stone, the Heel Stone, the Altar Stone, and others.

The Avenue begins at the entrance to Stonehenge. It leads away from the structure. It travels down a gentle slope for about 560 yards. Banks on both sides of the Avenue mark the way. The banks are about 40 feet apart.

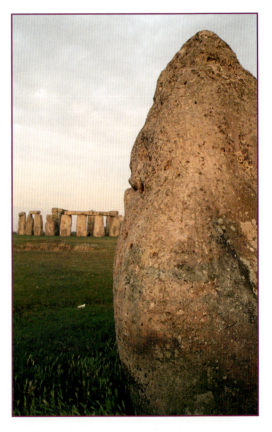

The Station Stones were probably put in place during Stonehenge III. However, some believe they were placed at the end of Phase I. Originally, four Station Stones formed a perfect rectangle. Now, only two survive. One of them has fallen. These sarsen stones are located just inside the bank. Unlike the stones in the center of the circle, the Station Stones were not shaped in any way.

▲ The fallen Slaughter Stone lies near the monument.

Also part of Phase III is the Slaughter Stone. This stone is located near the main entrance of the monument, beside the Avenue. It has fallen and lies on the ground. This partly smoothed sarsen stone is 21 feet long, 3 feet thick, and more than 7 feet wide.

Bumps and rusty red stains abound on the surface of the stone. At one time, people thought the red marks were bloodstains. That's how the stone got its name. However, the marks were caused by rainwater collecting in the holes. The water reacted with bits of iron in the stone, creating rust. The stone simply marked the entrance of Stonehenge. It was probably one of a pair of stones.

Farther along the Avenue is the **Heel Stone**. Many experts believe it was part of Phase I. It might have been the first sarsen stone placed at Stonehenge. The Heel Stone is about 8 feet wide and 16 feet tall. Another 4 feet of the stone is buried below ground. It is not shaped. Originally, the Heel Stone may have been paired with another stone. That stone is now missing. In 1979, another stone hole was found 12 feet to the northwest.

On the morning of the summer solstice, the sun rises behind the Heel Stone. The name of this stone probably came from the Greek word *helios*. It means "sun."

The **Altar Stone** is a smoothed blue-gray block of sandstone. It lies partly buried inside the trilithon horseshoe. It is 16 feet long, 3.5 feet wide, and 1.75 feet thick. It is not a bluestone or a sarsen, but it is a type of sandstone. Some experts think this stone came from Wales, near the Prescelly Mountains. Perhaps workers picked it up on their way to Stonehenge with a load of bluestones.

The Altar Stone, now fallen, got its name from its shape, not its use. The designers of Stonehenge placed this stone in the center of the bluestone horseshoe. It certainly must have had a special meaning to the designers. However, when the stone was upright, it could not have been used as an altar.

Two missing Station Stones once stood inside circular ditches. These two ditches are called the North Barrow and the South Barrow.

The last addition to Stonehenge appears to be two concentric circles. They are around the outside of the larger sarsen circle. These were labeled "Z" and "Y" holes. It seems that something was planned for them. However, the ancient builders, for reasons unknown to us, never went any further.

CHAPTER FIVE
The People of Stonehenge

The studies of Stonehenge are helping to unravel some mysteries. We have learned more about ancient people and how they lived. The information has been based on excavations, carbon dating, and other research.

Windmill Hill People, Beaker Folk, and Wessex People

As you know, Stonehenge was built over a period of about 1,500 years. During this time, several groups of people lived in the area. However, experts do not agree on which ones built Stonehenge.

Some experts believe that the Windmill Hill People built Stonehenge I. This group was a blend of local people and tribes from eastern England. Circles were an important part of their culture. The Windmill Hill People were named for a huge earth mound they built on Windmill Hill, near Stonehenge. They were mostly **nomads** and lived in small groups. That way, they could easily move to follow the seasons and migrating animals.

Most nomads did not grow crops or raise animals. Instead, they hunted, fished, and ate wild plants. However, the Windmill Hill People did plant wheat and some other crops. They also raised cattle, sheep, goats, and other animals.

Many experts believe that the Beaker Folk were involved in building Stonehenge II. Beaker Folk were named because of their pottery. How do we know this? Beaker-shaped drinking cups, along with weapons, were discovered in their graves. Beaker Folk were one of the first groups to use metal tools. They might have worshiped the sun.

▲ Ancient people created pottery in the shape of beakers.

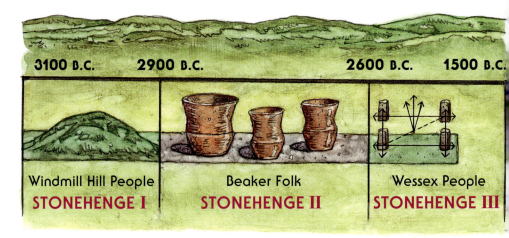

3100 B.C.	2900 B.C.	2600 B.C.	1500 B.C.
Windmill Hill People **STONEHENGE I**	Beaker Folk **STONEHENGE II**	Wessex People **STONEHENGE III**	

▲ The people of Stonehenge

Some believe that the Wessex People built Stonehenge III. The Wessex People lived during the Early Bronze Age. They were one of the most advanced cultures in that area at the time. Skillful traders, they controlled trade routes throughout England. Some members of the group became quite wealthy. The Wessex People were very skilled in mathematics. This skill probably helped them in the construction of Stonehenge III.

From Nomads to Farmers

For tools and weapons, nomads used flint, bone, and deer antlers. For shelter, they probably built huts at temporary campsites. They may have also used animal-skin tents. At first, they lived in areas covered with thick forests with little open grassland.

Later prehistoric cultures cleared some of the forests. They needed land for grazing cattle and raising pigs. They also kept dogs and goats. By the time Stonehenge was completed, these early British people were firmly rooted. They used established trade routes, wove their clothes and blankets, and produced advanced tools and weapons.

By 4000 B.C., more and more people were becoming farmers. Hunters had to live from day to day. However, farmers could build up a store of food. In time, this growing population began to affect the land. Forests were being replaced with open grassland and bushes.

By about 3000 B.C., much of the original forest had disappeared. The population continued to grow. People could be spared to work on community projects. Towns began to form.

▲ During the Stone Age, people used these kinds of tools every day.

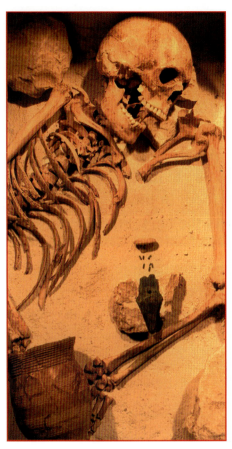

▲ This man was probably buried at about the same time when the bluestones were brought to Stonehenge. He is holding a pottery drinking cup. His bronze dagger was also buried with him.

No houses from this time survive near Stonehenge. However, houses built in other regions at this time were long and rectangular. They could have held a large family and its animals.

Life in prehistoric times was short. Forty percent of the population died before age 20. A 30-year-old person was considered quite old! In fact, it's likely that Stonehenge was built by teenagers.

Changing Customs

Sometime during the building of Stonehenge, a new custom began. Groups began to bury their dead, especially important people. They were buried under a mound of earth called a **barrow**. A drinking cup was buried with them. Sometimes a copper knife or a bow and arrows were included.

Scientists have made one strange discovery about the people of Stonehenge. They created very little trash. Diggers have uncovered pieces of flint, antler picks, and axes, but little else. Scientists love to examine the trash left behind by a group of people. It tells a lot about that group. A lack of trash means a lack of information for the scientists.

Some archaeologists have a theory about this lack of garbage. They believe that Stonehenge was considered sacred ground. Therefore, no trash could be left there. This monument clearly was a special place where people did not leave their garbage.

▼ The size and age of Stonehenge overwhelm most visitors.

Dedication to Stonehenge

It took an extremely long time to complete Stonehenge. A builder would see only a small amount of progress during his lifetime. Workers might toil every day for most of their lives just to shape, carry, and place a few stones. Were they slaves, forced to do the work? Were they deeply committed to a cause or a purpose? We just don't know. However, most experts believe that Stonehenge was built by people who wanted to build it. It was probably built by over 50 generations of such people.

Scientists believe the builders of Stonehenge knew a great deal about math and engineering. How else could they have placed the stones in those positions? How else could they have lifted and carried such huge stones? Remember that they did not have modern tools and machines.

We still have much to learn about the groups who built Stonehenge. Still, we can marvel at the planning, skill, time, and labor involved. Stonehenge was obviously very important to its creators, whoever they were.

CHAPTER SIX
The Purpose of Stonehenge

Why would Stone Age people from many generations take on such a huge project? This is still a difficult question. Scientists, archaeologists, historians, and astronomers have been trying to answer it for hundreds of years. If you like mysteries, this one is better than any solved by Sherlock Holmes!

We solve mysteries by studying clues. For Stonehenge, the only clues are the stones themselves, some crude tools, and some ancient objects dug out of the ground. We do not have much to go on.

Stonehenge is unique and colossal. What could its purpose have been?

The Druids

Do you remember John Aubrey and the Aubrey Holes? About 300 years ago, Aubrey was one of the first to suggest that ancient stone circles were really temples. He believed they were used by an ancient British tribe called the Druids. This group included doctors, priests, lawmakers, and philosophers. Some describe the early Druids as seekers of wisdom.

▲ Some theorize that the Druids built Stonehenge.

Since then, others have also come to believe that Stonehenge was built and used by Druids. One of them was William Stukeley (1687–1765). He is a well-known researcher of Stonehenge. Most of Stukeley's findings are respected. However, his ideas about the Druids are not.

We know that the Druids existed in Britain at about 250 B.C. Then they seemed to disappear until about 1781. That's when the Ancient Order of Druids formed. This group first visited Stonehenge in 1905.

This would mean that the Druids first appeared many years after Stonehenge had already been abandoned. There is no evidence linking the two things. Still, modern Druids insist they have a connection to Stonehenge. Some of them travel to Stonehenge at the summer solstice, the longest day of the year.

Early Folklore

People told many stories about the purpose of Stonehenge. Some believed that the monument began as a circle of dancing giants. Then they were turned into stone. A few believe that Stonehenge was created by aliens from outer space.

Geoffrey of Monmouth was a writer long ago. He was probably the first to write about the purpose of Stonehenge. In 1136, he concluded that Stonehenge was the work of Merlin the

▼ Merlin was a character in the ancient tales about King Arthur.

▲ Stonehenge beneath the phases of the moon

Magician. Merlin was the wizard of King Arthur's court. However, if Merlin built Stonehenge, it would have had to happen 2,000 to 3,000 years later than the construction of Stonehenge.

Some say the bluestones were magical healing stones. Merlin brought them to Stonehenge from Ireland.

Geoffrey of Monmouth's ideas remained popular until the seventeenth century. Then King James I hired Inigo Jones to look into Stonehenge. Jones was England's first major architect and designer. After studying Stonehenge, he decided it was a Roman building. He thought it had been created to serve the Roman gods. Jones was an Englishman. Still, he refused to believe that the British people could have created such a monument. He thought they did not have the skill to build Stonehenge.

Jones overlooked one important fact. Stonehenge was built long before the Romans invaded Britain. In fact, in A.D. 61, the Romans reportedly tore down part of Stonehenge.

Astronomy and Stonehenge

For centuries, people have studied the positions of the stones. Some believe that the site for Stonehenge was chosen because of its relationship to the movements of the sun and the moon. Some think the huge stones were arranged to predict comets, eclipses, and other events in the sky. The sun and moon were very important to ancient people. Anyone who could predict their movements was respected and even worshiped.

Another idea is that the stones were designed to serve as a calendar. They would help measure the passage of time. In fact, there are 30 sarsens in the circle. Could they stand for the days of the month? We don't know for sure.

More recently, researchers have studied the Station Stones. They think the positions of these stones are important. They mark the most northerly and southerly place on the horizon where the sun and the moon rise and set.

In 1963, a British man named C.A. Newham focused on the position of Stonehenge on the surface of Earth. At Stonehenge, the rising and setting of the sun and moon are at right angles to one another. This occurs, Newham said, only at Stonehenge. He believed that was why this site was chosen for the monument.

According to Newham, ancient astronomers would stand in the center of Stonehenge. As they watched the sun or moon set, they would note its position. Then they could tell when the sun or moon had reached the extreme limit of its orbit. They could inform their followers that a new cycle was about to begin.

In the 1960s, British astronomer Gerald Hawkins agreed with Newham. Hawkins was a professor of astronomy at Boston University. He studied the patterns of the stones and the Aubrey Holes. He believed the patterns related to events in the sky. Hawkins concluded that the site had been an observatory. He believed it was also used long ago to predict eclipses.

To prove his theory, Hawkins used a modern computer. He entered the known movements of the moon over Stonehenge in 1554 B.C. Then he figured out what would happen if small stones were placed inside certain Aubrey Holes and moved every year. According to Hawkins, the stones would reach the hole in front of the Heel Stone in the same year as an eclipse of the moon. However, some archaeologists do not agree with Hawkins' theories. They

▲ This is how Stonehenge looks today. Many stones have fallen or are missing. Some of the remaining bluestones are broken stumps.

believe this system is too complex for the Early Bronze Age society of Britain.

Pursuing Purpose

Some people think that the pattern of all the stones had a purpose. It predicted the best times for planting and harvesting. Knowing these times is very important to farmers. These times are tied to the summer solstice, when the sun is at its highest point.

The purpose of Stonehenge could have been any number of things—or a combination of them. It might have been a religious temple or a place to observe the stars. Some believe it was a gigantic calendar. Others think it was a marketplace or a meeting place.

All of these theories are mostly guesses. Prehistoric people left no written records for us to study. Even today's modern technology has not unlocked many of the secrets of Stonehenge. Its purpose still lies buried beneath the tons of rock that make it such a world treasure.

Stonehenge stands for us to investigate, explore, and marvel. We can try to imagine what it would have been like to work on such a huge project—a project which was not finished in any one individual's lifetime! Think about what dedication it took for these people to commit to their community—for a purpose they would never see complete. How would you have felt being such a person?

CHAPTER SEVEN
Other Stone Circles

Many other stone circles dot England, Wales, Scotland, and Ireland. In fact, Stonehenge is part of a network of structures built over thousands of years. Many, but not all of them, are formed in circles. The network includes hundreds of burial mounds.

In some of these circles, the stones were placed upright, like those at Stonehenge. Other circles are formed from smaller stones piled on top of larger ones. However, only at Stonehenge were the stones brought from great distances. Only there were the stones trimmed and shaped.

Even more circles were created of wood. However, the wood in these has rotted. Much information about them has been lost to us. Often the only evidence of ancient monuments appears in the way crops grow on the land. Wheat is darker when it grows on land that has been dug up. It is also darker over spots that once held posts or walls. Wheat is lighter when it grows on land that has not been disturbed. Scientists in planes flying over these areas can see these patterns. When they find an unexplained pattern, they know where to begin digging.

Robin Hood's Ball

One ancient circle was easy to locate. It is only 2.5 miles from Stonehenge. It was built well before Stonehenge, about 3900 B.C. It is called Robin Hood's Ball; however, it has nothing to do with Robin Hood. It consists of two earthen circles of ditches, one inside the other. As far as we know, this ancient circle did not include stones or wood. It is the largest monument to survive from this period.

Scientists have uncovered much information by digging in ditches and walls like the ones at Robin Hood's Ball. What do they find that tells them more about the places and the people? They often find the remains of feasts, for example. This includes pieces of pottery and animal bones. They also find human bones. Ancient people, it appears, spent a good part of their time close to their dead.

Durrington Walls

Two miles east of Stonehenge lie Durrington Walls. When they were built, these walls were 30 feet high. Inside them were two separate circles formed by oak posts. Other circles might have existed inside the walls, too. The walls enclose a much larger area than Stonehenge. They are about one third of a mile across. Part of the area might have had a roof at one time.

No one is sure of the purpose of Durrington Walls. However, they were built about the same time as Stonehenge I. Much flint, animal bones, and pottery have

▲ Stone circles and barrows (burial chambers) were built throughout England, Ireland, and Europe.

been uncovered here, but no human bones. Why do you think no human bones were discovered? It probably did not serve as a burial site. Some people think the site was a shelter for the Stonehenge workers. Nevertheless, there is no evidence that this is true.

Woodhenge

Very near Durrington Walls, but much smaller, is Woodhenge. Woodhenge was discovered in photographs taken from an airplane. At one time, Woodhenge consisted of six rings of timbers, one inside another. The timbers are gone, of course. However, their holes have been marked with short concrete posts. Woodhenge is slightly smaller than Stonehenge. It was probably built about 2000 B.C. In some ways, it is like the "timber monument" of Stonehenge. However, when its posts rotted, Woodhenge was abandoned and never rebuilt.

Arrowheads and other objects have been found in pits here. They show that this place was used for some purpose long before the circles were built. Pieces of human bone suggest that it was a burial site.

Barrows

Many of the surviving monuments near Stonehenge are barrows. A barrow is a burial mound. The first barrows were long group graves. Early people buried their dead together. There were often as many as 40 people buried in one mound. Most of the long barrows

▲ An example of barrows near Stonehenge

▲ Henges and barrows in England, Wales, Scotland, and Ireland

near Stonehenge face toward the sunrise. Ancient people believed that the sun was very important in their lives.

Later groups buried each person in a separate, round mound. Often gold, amber, and bronze objects have been found in the mounds. What do these objects tell us about the culture of the people at that time? The objects, like those in Egyptian tombs, indicated the importance of the person. Apparently, it was a great honor to be buried near Stonehenge. However, no one was allowed to be buried on the site itself.

The Cursus

Near Stonehenge is a path that runs east and west for nearly two miles. It is a slightly raised platform between two banks and ditches. It was first recognized by William Stukeley, a British researcher and expert on Stonehenge. Because it looked like a place for a race, Stukeley called it the cursus. The word cursus is taken from a Latin word meaning "racecourse." We are still not sure of the real purpose of the cursus. It apparently was built around 3500 B.C. That was even before Stonehenge I.

Other cursuses were also built in the region around Stonehenge. Some of them point to the sunset at midsummer. Others point to the sunset at midwinter. The Stonehenge cursus points to sunrise at the **equinox**. On this day of the year, there is an equal amount of day and night.

▲ The round, brown megalith and nearby round barrows are easy to see from an airplane.

CHAPTER EIGHT
Stonehenge Today and Tomorrow

"When you first reach the area, you are astounded that you can see it from so far away," says Lillie Plowman. She is a marketing specialist from Missouri. She visited Stonehenge with her husband, Jeremy, who is a high school teacher, in 2001. "Then you realize how many thousands of people are there to see this incredible site as well. Your excitement builds as you get closer to its magnificence and beauty. But you don't really realize the size of it until you are actually there—up close. Even from a distance it doesn't appear to be as large as it is."

"The landscape around Stonehenge makes you wonder about the past civilizations living there," says Jeremy. "The knowledge that the builders of Stonehenge must have had in regards to astronomy, architecture, and engineering is astonishing. It was ahead of its time in so many ways. Imagine the number of people needed to build this and the length of time it took. And trying to figure out why the stones were laid out in such patterns causes one to really think."

▲ Sunset at Stonehenge

"It would have been amazing to have been around that society during the time of history when this was built," adds Lillie. "Imagine all the knowledge, community, and intelligence that was needed to build this."

Stonehenge Struggles

Stonehenge has endured thousands of years of use and abuse. In medieval times, peasants and stonemasons reportedly removed some of the stones. They used them to make houses and bridges. For many years, visitors were allowed to roam around the stones. They could even climb on them. Some people thought the stones had magic powers. They chipped off pieces to take home. Even in the nineteenth century, nearby hotels encouraged visitors to take pieces of stone as souvenirs. The hotels even rented out hammers!

For centuries, the area around Stonehenge was isolated. Now two roads bring visitors to the monument. About 800,000 people visit every year. They have worn down the monument.

At one time, Stonehenge was privately owned. Today, it is managed by an agency called English Heritage. This government body helps to preserve this national treasure.

To deal with the increasing number of visitors, the Stonehenge Master Plan was created. The plan was the result of nearly eight years of discussion. It states that roads around the monument will be closed or removed to cut down on traffic. A new visitor center will be built.

▲ As late as the 1960s, people climbed the stones to watch ceremonies.

▲ Today, Stonehenge is a stone's throw from a busy highway.

A new transit system will take visitors to within walking distance of the stones.

In addition, the land around the monument will all be grass. Cattle will graze there. All modern features, including fences, will be removed. Visitors will be able to appreciate Stonehenge as it was centuries ago.

A Director's Thoughts

Clews Everard is the director of Stonehenge. She points out that we have learned much about Stonehenge. Still, much more remains a mystery. "No one really knows why it was built or why it was erected in that location," she says. "What we do know is that it was an amazing feat of engineering.

"The story of Stonehenge is not just about a prehistoric monument that is located in Britain. It's a wonderful chronicle of how, over hundreds of years, people toiled to carve the stones after they had been transported from many miles away…. The builders would have found the stones in a rough state. Then they would have worked tirelessly to get them shaped and finished. Beyond that, there were the lintels that they put on the top of each sarsen, using a very sophisticated system….

"All of this includes such unbelievable feats of engineering," says Everard. "How did they manage to carve the stones so precisely? How did they manage to erect the whole structure so intricately? Even with its disintegration, it has withstood centuries!

"There is no doubt about one thing though. There is an enduring and intense fascination for Stonehenge that exists today, even after thousands of years. It is truly one of the most prestigious and majestic sites in Britain—one that has been enjoyed by people all over the world."

Visitors cannot help but be impressed with Stonehenge. "I think the most appealing thing about Stonehenge is the mystery," says an American visitor. "No one seems to know what it was built to do. I would love to know its real purpose, but I don't think we'll ever know for sure. That is, unless someone invents time travel. I could describe it in one word—awesome!"

GLOSSARY

Altar Stone (**awl•**tahr **stohn**) a blue-gray block of sandstone at Stonehenge. It is shaped like an altar.

bank (**bank**) a mound or pile of soil

barrow (**bar•**oh) a large mound of earth that lies on top of a burial chamber

carbon dating (**kar•**buhn **day•**ting) see "radiocarbon dating" below

ceremonial (sehr•uh•**moh•**nee•uhl) having to do with an act of celebration

corridor (**kor•**i•duhr) an area like a hallway

ditch (**ditch**) a long narrow area that has been dug

down (**down**) gently rolling plains located in southern England

dressing (**drehs•**ing) shaping a stone in some way

equinox (**ee•**kwuh•noks) a time of equal parts of day and equal parts of night. Equinoxes occur around March 21 and September 23.

excavation (ehk•skuh•**vay•**shuhn) a cavity that has been created by digging or scooping

Heel Stone (**heel stohn**) a sarsen stone at Stonehenge named after the Greek word for sun.

igneous (**ig•**nee•uhs) formed by fire or great heat under the earth's surface or in volcanoes

lintels (**lin•**tuhlz) horizontal pieces placed across the tops of two upright pieces

megalith (**mehg**•uh•lith) comes from the Greek word meaning "great stone"

Neolithic (Nee•uh•**lith**•ik) the latest period of the Stone Age, usually between about 8000 B.C. and about 5000 B.C.

nomads (**noh**•madz) people who move from place to place. Nomads were usually searching for food, water, and better weather.

obelisk (**ob**•uh•lisk) a pillar of stone, particularly one that was built as a monument. It has a square base with sides that taper to a point, like a pyramid.

radiocarbon dating (ray•dee•oh•**kar**•buhn **day**•ting) also called carbon dating; a way to determine the age of organic remains; based on measuring the amounts of carbon in a living thing after it dies

sedimentary (sehd•uh•**mehn**•tuh•ree) formed from sand or other matter set down by wind or water

sledges (**slej**•ez) strong, heavy sleds

solstice (**sol**•stis) either the longest or shortest day of the year, about June 21 and December 21

trilithons (try•**lith**•onz) pairs of upright stones topped with a lintel

BIBLIOGRAPHY

Balfour, Michael. *Stonehenge and Its Mysteries*. New York: Charles Scribner's Sons, 1979.

Branley, Franklyn M. *The Mystery of Stonehenge*. (Raintree Childrens Books) New York: Thomas Y. Crowell, 1969.

Brown, David J. *How Things Were Built*. New York: Random House, 1992.

Burl, Aubrey. *Great Stone Circles*. New Haven and London: Yale University Press, 1999.

Castleden, Rodney. *The Stonehenge People*. London and New York: Routledge and Kegan Paul Ltd., 1987.

Ceserani, Gian Paolo. *Grand Constructions*. New York: Putnam Pub Group, 1983.

Chippindale, Christopher. *Stonehenge Complete*. New York: Thames and Hudson, 1994.

Chippindale, Christopher, Paul Devereux, Peter Fowler, Rhys Jones, and Tim Sebastian. *Who Owns Stonehenge?* London: B.T. Batsford, 1990.

Corbishley, Mike. *The World of Architectural Wonders*. Chicago: National Textbook Corporation, 1996.

Cowan, Henry J. (Editor*). The World's Greatest Buildings: Masterpieces of Architecture and Engineering* (Time-Life Guides). New York: Time Life, 1992.

Hawkins, Gerald. *Stonehenge Decoded*. (A Delta Book). New York: Dell Publications Company, 1965.

————. *Beyond Stonehenge*. New York: Harper and Row, 1973.

Lyon, Nancy. *The Mystery of Stonehenge*. Milwaukee: Contemporary Perspectives, 1977.

Mass, Wendy. *Stonehenge* (Building History Series). San Diego, CA: Lucent Books, 1998.

Osborne, Ken (Editor). *Stonehenge and Neighbouring Monuments*. London: English Heritage, 1995.

Souden, David. *Stonehenge Revealed*. New York: Facts on File, 1997.

Stover, Leon E. and Bruce Kraig. *Stonehenge: The Indo-European Heritage*. Chicago: Nelson-Hall, 1978.

Westwood, Jennifer (Editor). *The Atlas of Mysterious Places: The World's Unexplained Sacred Sites, Symbolic Landscapes, Ancient Cities, and Lost Lands*. Santa Barbara, CA: Grove Press, 1987.

WEB SITES

Earth Mysteries: Stonehenge
http://witcombe.sbc.edu/earthmysteries/EMStonehenge.html

Mystic Places – Stonehenge
http://exn.ca/mysticplaces/Preservation.cfm

Stonehenge and the Druids
http://witcombe.sbc.edu/earthmysteries/EMStonehengeC.html

Welcome to Stonehenge
http://www.fortunecity.com/roswell/blavatsky/123/stnhng.html

Stonehenge:
http://www.activemind.com/Mysterious/Topics/Stonehenge/
http://www.stonehenge.co.uk/Stonehenge/stonehenge.htm
http://www.plus44.com/heritage/stoneheng/stonehen.html
http://www.stonehenge-avebury.net/stnhngeinfo.html
http://www.encyclopedia.com/articles/12364.html
http://encarta.msn.com/find/Concise.asp?&pg=2&ti=00767000
http://www.britannia.com/history/h7.html
http://unmuseum.mus.pa.us/stonehen.htm

INDEX